TAKE THAT
PROGRESS

D1649861

© 2010 by Faber Music Ltd
First published by Faber Music Ltd in 2010
Bloomsbury House 74–77 Great Russell Street London WC1B 3DA

Arrangements: Alex Davis & Olly Weeks
Editor: Lucy Holliday

Photography: Nadav Kander
Design and Art Direction: Studio Fury

Management: Jonathan Wild at 10 Management
Robbie Williams Management: ie music

Printed in England by Caligraving Ltd
All rights reserved

The text paper used in this publication is a virgin fibre product that
is manufactured in the EU. The wood fibre used is only sourced from
managed forests using sustainable forestry principles.
This paper is 100% recyclable

ISBN10: 0-571-53596-8
EAN13: 978-0-571-53596-5

Reproducing this music in any form is illegal and forbidden by the
Copyright, Designs and Patents Act, 1988

To buy Faber Music publications or to find out about the full range of titles
available, please contact your local music retailer or Faber Music sales enquiries:

Faber Music Ltd, Burnt Mill, Elizabeth Way, Harlow, CM20 2HX England
Tel: +44(0)1279 82 89 82 Fax: +44(0)1279 82 89 83
sales@fabermusic.com fabermusic.com

THE FLOOD

Words and Music by Gary Barlow, Howard Donald,
Jason Orange, Mark Owen and Robbie Williams

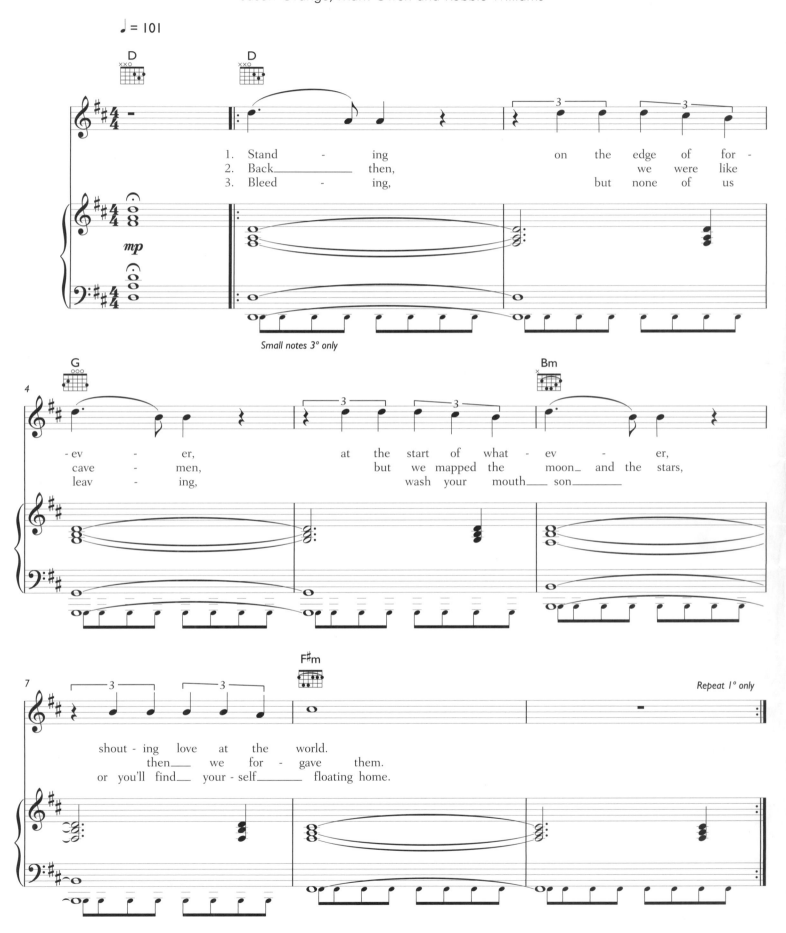

1. Stand - ing on the edge of for -
2. Back then, we were like
3. Bleed - ing, but none of us

- ev - er, at the start of what - ev - er,
cave - men, but we mapped the moon and the stars,
leav - ing, wash your mouth son

Small notes 3° only

shout - ing love at the world.
then we for - gave them.
or you'll find your - self floating home.

Repeat 1° only

© 2010 EMI Music Publishing Ltd, Farrell Music Ltd/Robbie Williams,
Universal Music Publishing MGB Ltd and Sony/ATV Music Publishing (UK) Ltd

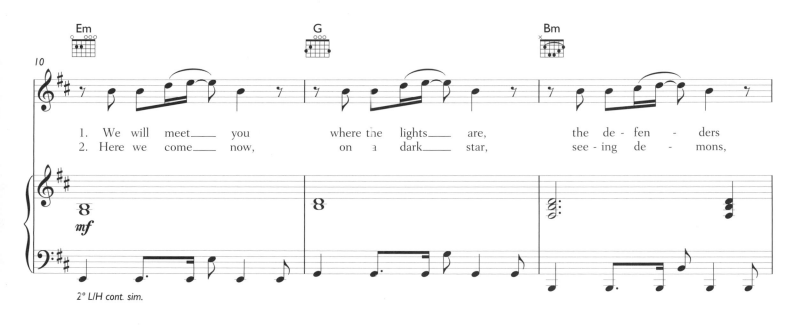

1. We will meet____ you where the lights____ are, the de - fen - ders
2. Here we come____ now, on a dark____ star, see - ing de - mons,

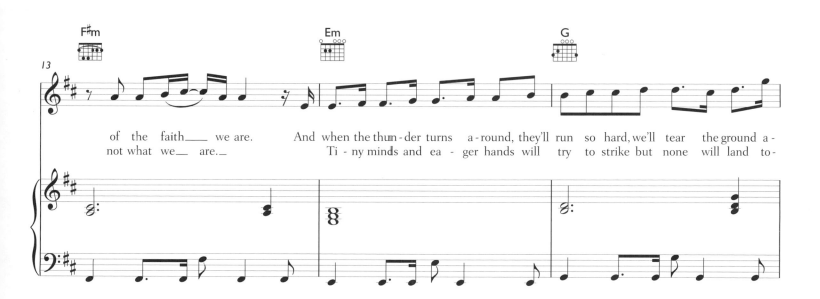

of the faith____ we are. And when the thun - der turns a - round, they'll run so hard, we'll tear the ground a -
not what we____ are.____ Ti - ny minds and ea - ger hands will try to strike but none will land to -

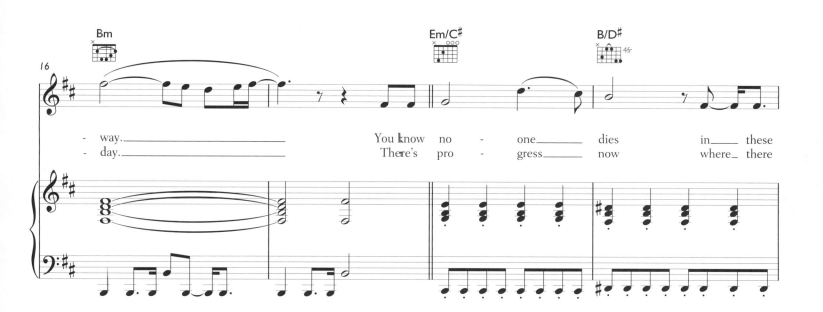

- way.____ You know no - one____ dies in____ these
- day.____ There's pro - gress____ now where____ there

⊕ **Coda**

Now we'll ne-ver dance a - gain._____ Oh_____ ah, oh_____ ah,

oh_____ ah, oh_____ ah. Oh_____ ah,

oh_____ ah, oh_____ ah, oh_____ ah.

SOS

Words and Music by Gary Barlow, Howard Donald,
Jason Orange, Mark Owen and Robbie Williams

© 2010 EMI Music Publishing Ltd, Farrell Music Ltd/Robbie Williams,
Universal Music Publishing MGB Ltd and Sony/ATV Music Publishing (UK) Ltd

(1.) five mi-nute warn-ing for di-vine in-ter-ven-tion, with the sa-tel-lites fall-ing, pre-pare for a-scen-sion. Un-der
(2.) five se-cond warn-ing for di-vine in-ter-ven-tion, and the sa-tel-lites are fall-ing, pre-pare for a-scen-sion. As the

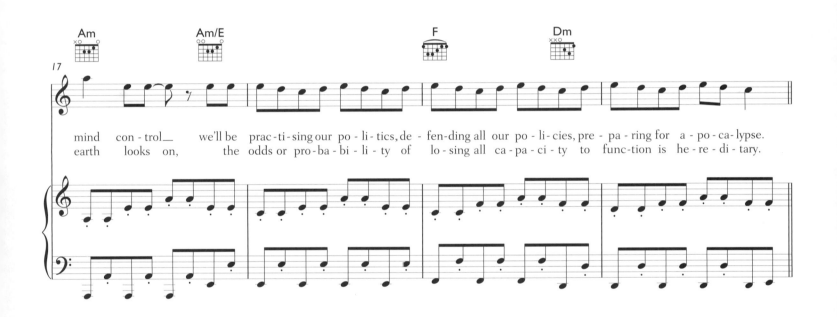

mind con-trol__ we'll be prac-ti-sing our po-li-tics, de-fen-ding all our po-li-cies, pre-pa-ring for a-po-ca-lypse.
earth looks on, the odds or pro-ba-bi-li-ty of lo-sing all ca-pa-ci-ty to func-tion is he-re-di-tary.

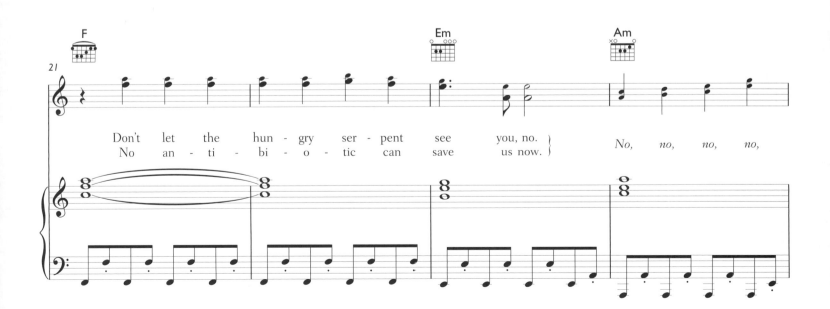

Don't let the hun-gry ser-pent see you, no. }
No an-ti-bi-o-tic can save us now. }

No, no, no, no,

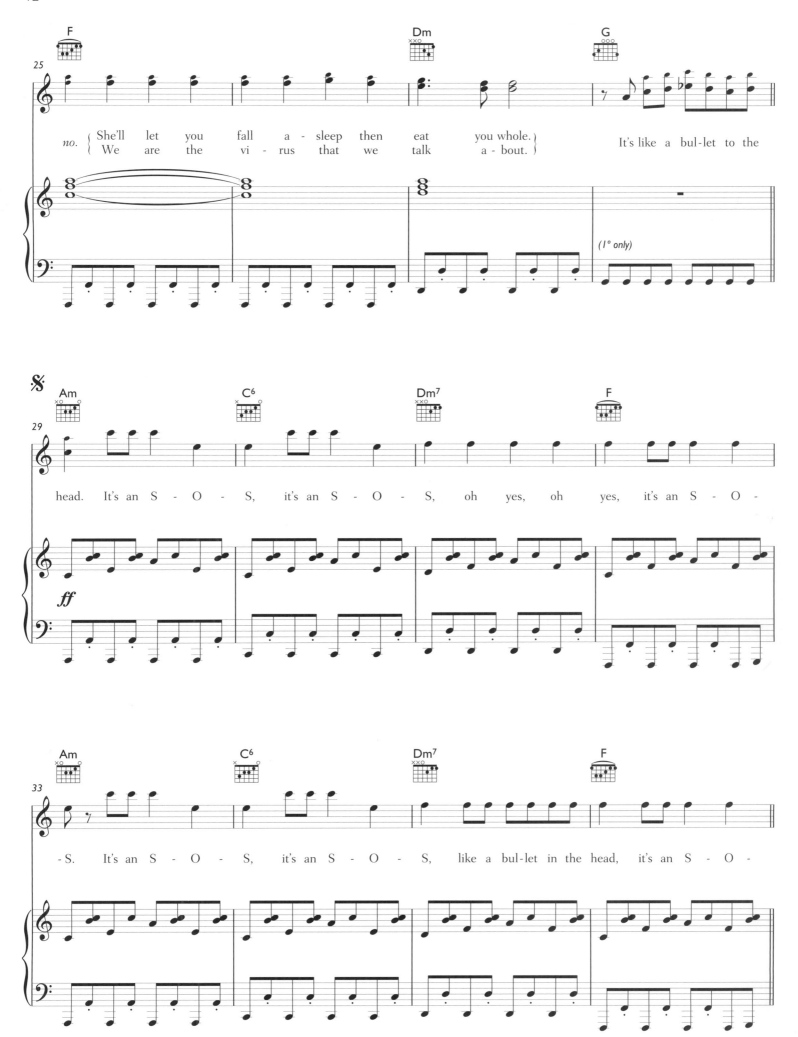

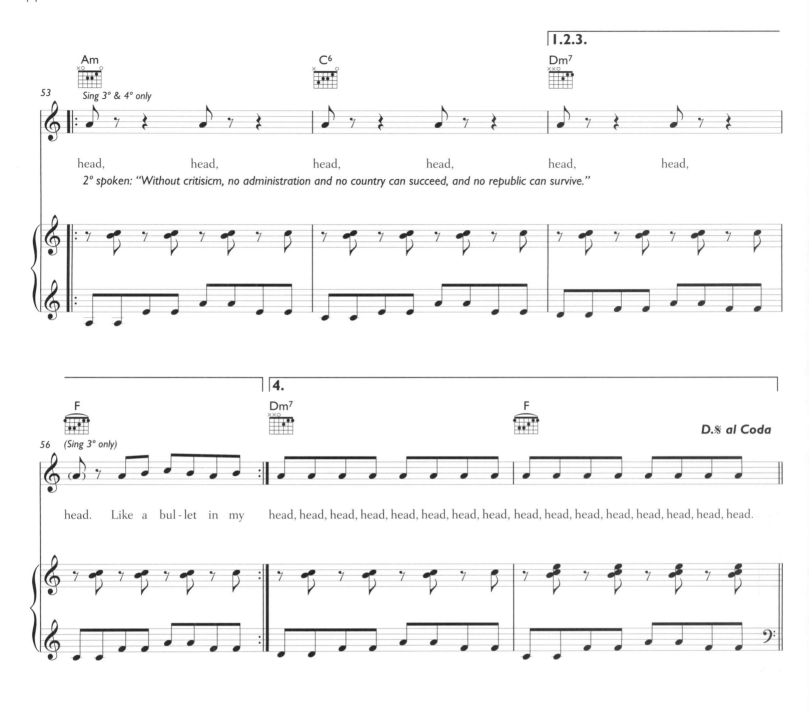

1.2.3.

head, head, head, head, head, head,

2° spoken: "Without critisicm, no administration and no country can succeed, and no republic can survive."

4.

D.% al Coda

(Sing 3° only)

head. Like a bul-let in my head, head, head, head, head, head, head, head, head, head, head, head, head, head, head, head.

Coda

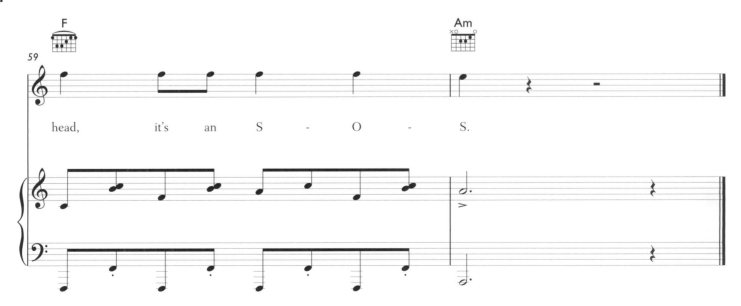

head, it's an S - O - S.

WAIT

Words and Music by Gary Barlow, Howard Donald,
Jason Orange, Mark Owen and Robbie Williams

© 2010 EMI Music Publishing Ltd, Farrell Music Ltd/Robbie Williams,
Universal Music Publishing MGB Ltd and Sony/ATV Music Publishing (UK) Ltd

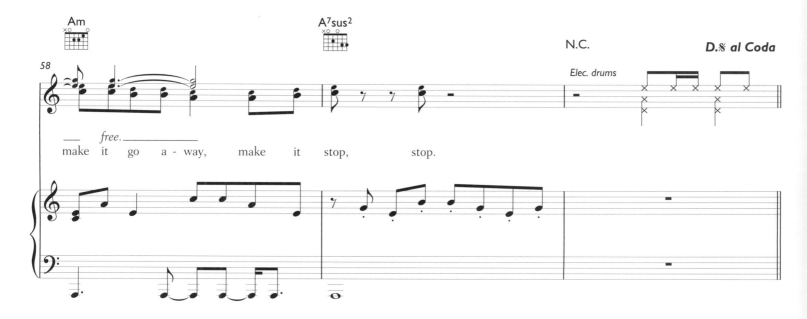

free.

make it go a - way, make it stop, stop.

Coda

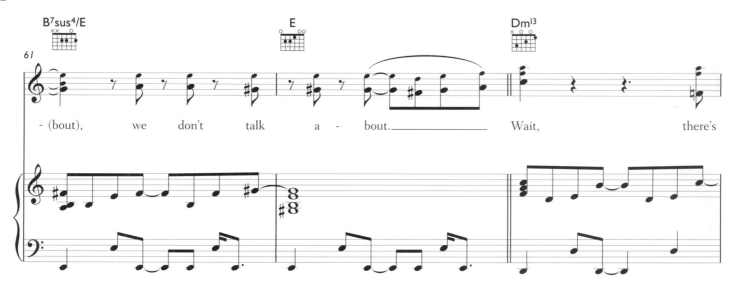

- (bout), we don't talk a - bout._____ Wait, there's

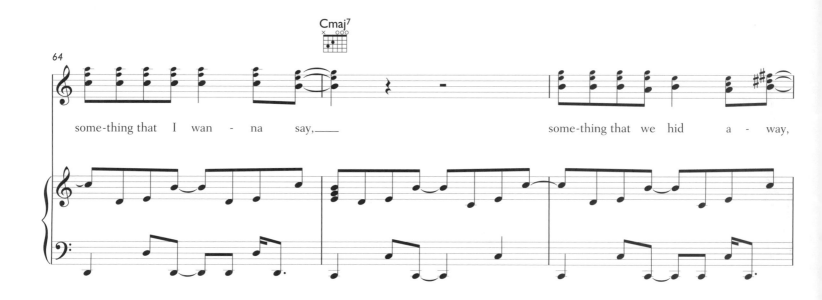

some-thing that I wan - na say,___ some-thing that we hid a - way,

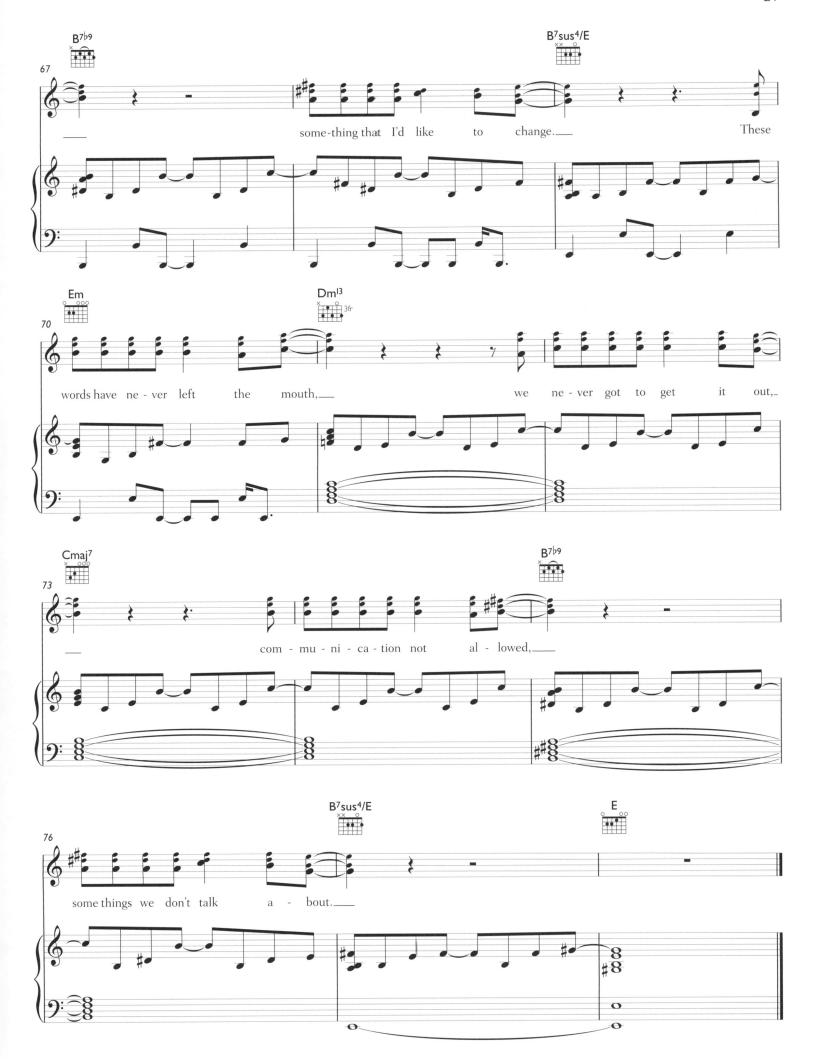

KIDZ

Words and Music by Gary Barlow, Howard Donald,
Jason Orange, Mark Owen and Robbie Williams

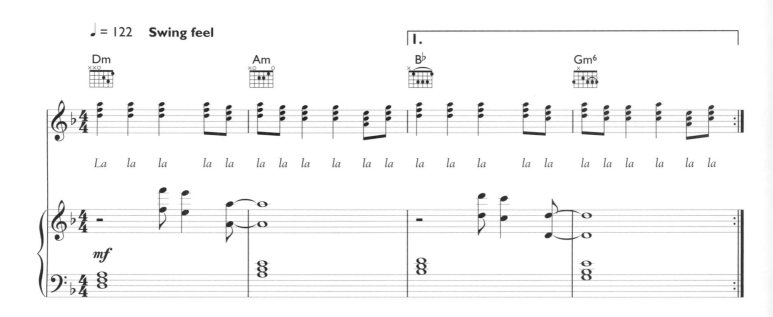

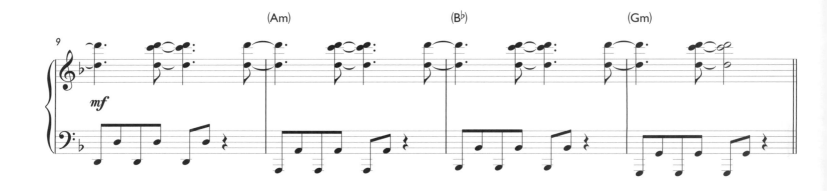

© 2010 EMI Music Publishing Ltd, Farrell Music Ltd/Robbie Williams,
Universal Music Publishing MGB Ltd and Sony/ATV Music Publishing (UK) Ltd

PRETTY THINGS

Words and Music by Gary Barlow, Howard Donald,
Jason Orange, Mark Owen and Robbie Williams

1. Dumb down, let your cra-zy out, boys go cra-zy o-ver you.
2. They're still out there some-where, ma-king men feel this

___ way.
At Ful-ham Broad-way sta-tion,

Grip like a New York win-dow clean-er,

© 2010 EMI Music Publishing Ltd, Farrell Music Ltd/Robbie Williams,
Universal Music Publishing MGB Ltd and Sony/ATV Music Publishing (UK) Ltd

D.% al Coda

Does she tell you what she wants? Can you give her what she needs?

Coda

Ob - vi - ous - ly cun - ning - ly wo - man - ly. All those pret - ty things,

God bless the pret - ty things._____

HAPPY NOW

Words and Music by Gary Barlow, Howard Donald,
Jason Orange, Mark Owen and Robbie Williams

1. I get the feel-ing that we are be-ing lied to, there's a surge in my psy-cho-sis ev-'ry
(2.) mer-cy of un-want-ed e - mo - tions,__ where no-thing mat-ters, be-neath my thoughts,__ be-
(3.) back of the club__ and so a-fraid__ to speak, 'cos I'm__ not like these peo-ple and these people are

turn of the screw. And I'm__ half a-wake in pais-ley print, I can
-neath my thoughts is where it hap-pens. Su-per hea-vy e - le - ments__ em-brace__ me,____
not like__ me.__ Su-per hea-vy e - le - ments__ up-grade me,____

© 2010 EMI Music Publishing Ltd, Farrell Music Ltd/Robbie Williams,
Universal Music Publishing MGB Ltd and Sony/ATV Music Publishing (UK) L-d

see the world clear-ly but I have to squint. I am a su-per-son-ic spe-ce-min,
su-per hea-vy e-le-ments_ re-place_ me. Was it a po-si-tive ex-pe-ri-ment_
su-per-so-nic e-le-ments_ a-maze_ me. Your o-pi-nion is ir-rel-le-vant,_

a mi-nor mi-ra-cle of me-di-cine.
to be in-de-fi-nite-ly de-ce-dant.
I was built to be mag-ni-fi-cent.

2. I'm at the

And they checked
And they checked

my pulse_ and it gave_ them hope that there was_ no truth to what was wrote. Give me half

scratched the sur - face of my__ de - si - re, in the world of dreams I'm a fre - quent fly - er.

Su-per hea-vy e - le-ments em - brace me. Su-per hea-vy e - le-ments.

N.C.

D.% al Coda

Coda

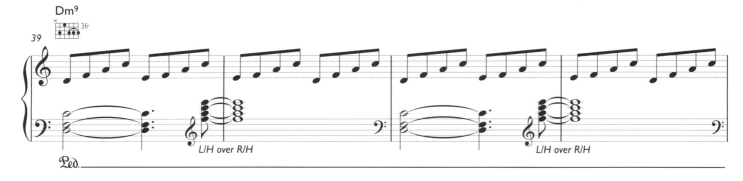

L/H over R/H

L/H over R/H

L/H over R/H

UNDERGROUND MACHINE

Words and Music by Gary Barlow, Howard Donald,
Jason Orange, Mark Owen and Robbie Williams

1. I,_____ I'm just a piece of your pie____ chart,
(2.) _____ I wish that beg - gars were choo - sers...

you're in a room_ with a rock__ star,__ on - ly I__ play the good
un - load__ my love like a loot - er,__ I need some gas and a kick

© 2010 EMI Music Publishing Ltd, Farrell Music Ltd/Robbie Williams,
Universal Music Publishing MGB Ltd and Sony/ATV Music Publishing (UK) Ltd

WHAT DO YOU WANT FROM ME?

Words and Music by Gary Barlow, Howard Donald,
Jason Orange, Mark Owen and Robbie Williams

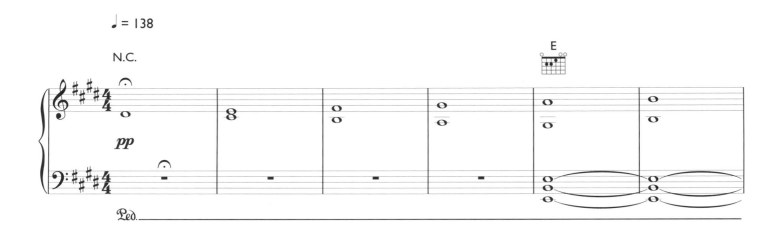

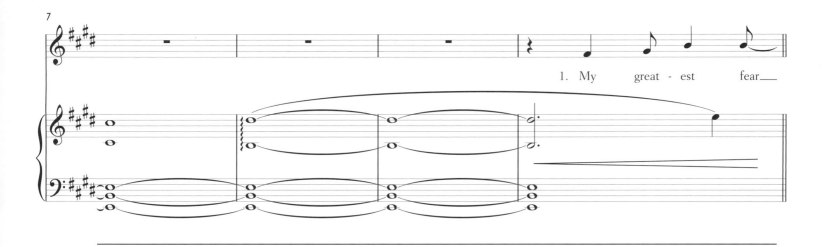

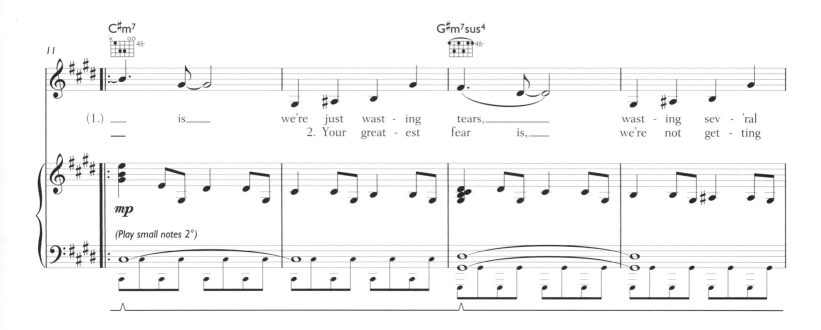

© 2010 EMI Music Publishing Ltd, Farrell Music Ltd/Robbie Williams,
Universal Music Publishing MGB Ltd and Sony/ATV Music Publishing (UK) Ltd

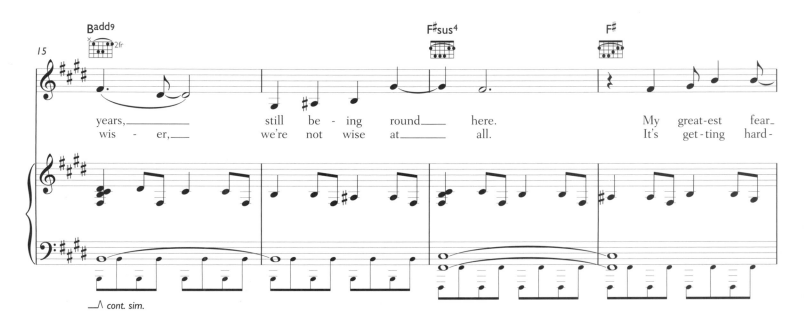

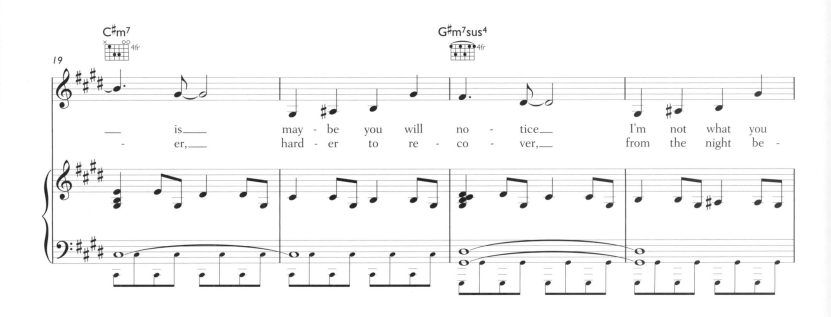

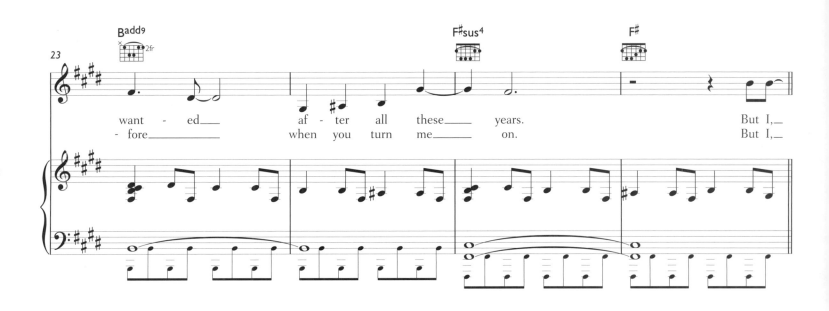

AFFIRMATION

Words and Music by Gary Barlow, Howard Donald,
Jason Orange, Mark Owen and Robbie Williams

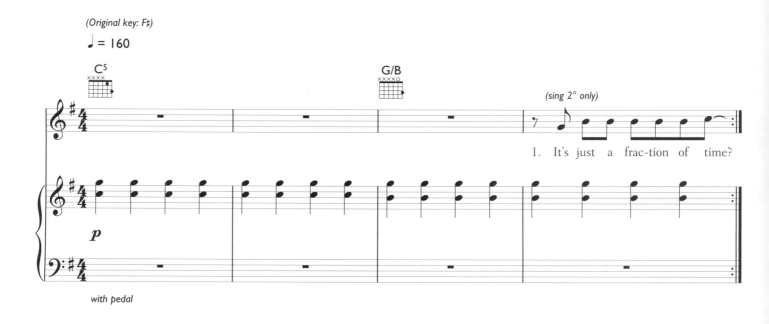

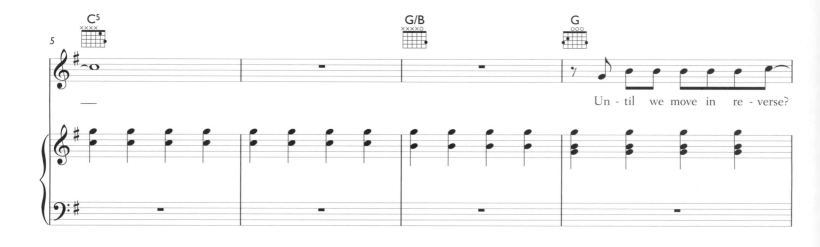

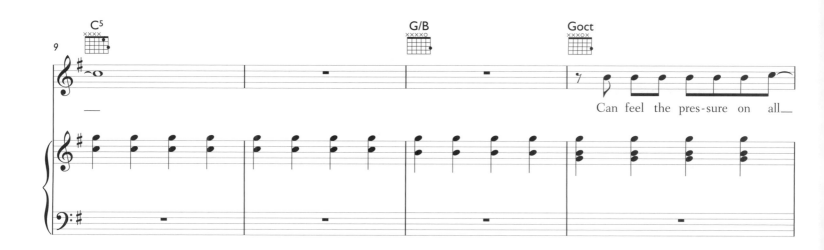

© 2010 EMI Music Publishing Ltd, Farrell Music Ltd/Robbie Williams,
Universal Music Publishing MGB Ltd and Sony/ATV Music Publishing (UK) Ltd

EIGHT LETTERS

Words and Music by Gary Barlow, Howard Donald,
Jason Orange, Mark Owen and Robbie Williams

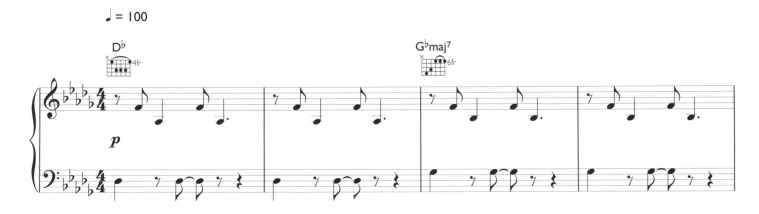

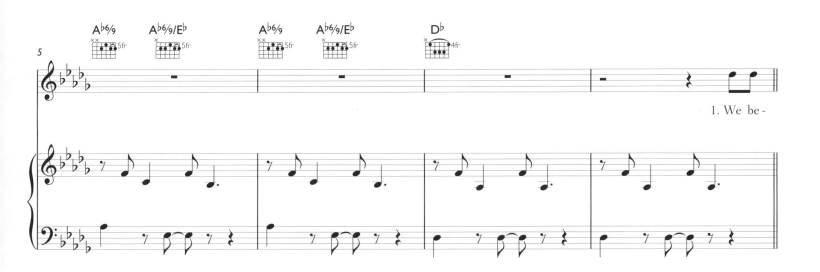

1. We be-

-came the pa-rade on the streets that we_ once cleaned, ex-pen-da-ble sol-diers
(2.) out-side_ forces did-n't make it ea-sy, so I thought I'd go be-

(Omit small notes 1°)

© 2010 EMI Music Publishing Ltd, Farrell Music Ltd/Robbie Williams,
Universal Music Publishing MGB Ltd and Sony/ATV Music Publishing (UK) Ltd

FLOWERBED

Words and Music by Gary Barlow, Howard Donald,
Jason Orange, Mark Owen and Robbie Williams

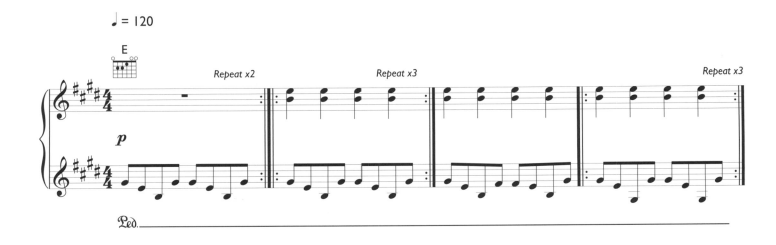

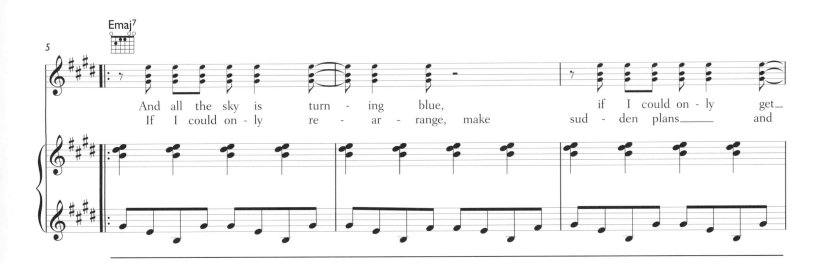

And all the sky is turn-ing blue, if I could on-ly get
If I could on-ly re-ar-range, make sud-den plans and

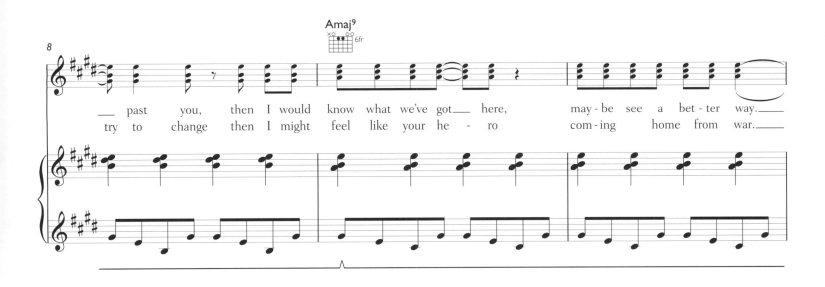

___ past you, then I would know what we've got___ here, may-be see a bet-ter way.___
try to change then I might feel like your he-ro com-ing home from war.___

© 2010 EMI Music Publishing Ltd, Farrell Music Ltd/Robbie Williams,
Universal Music Publishing MGB Ltd and Sony/ATV Music Publishing (UK) Ltd